Garfield

Happy Landings

JIM DAVIS

RAVETTE BOOKS

First published by Ravette Books Limited 1989
Reprinted 1989, 1990, 1991 (twice), 1993

Printed and bound in Great Britain
for Ravette Books Limited,
8 Clifford Street, London W1X 1RB
An Egmont Company
by Cox & Wyman Ltd, Reading

ISBN 1 85304 105 X

© 1988 United Feature Syndicate, Inc.

© 1988 United Feature Syndicate, Inc.

YOU WATCH A LOT OF T.V. DO YOU KNOW THAT, GARFIELD?

I CAN'T READ. WHAT'S YOUR EXCUSE?

4-19

JIM DAVIS

© 1988 United Feature Syndicate, Inc.

4-21

JIM DAVIS

AUNT GUSSIE WILL TAKE CARE OF YOU WHILE I'M IN THE HOSPITAL HAVING MY TONSILS REMOVED

AUNT GUSSIE?! OH, GREAT!

OH, COME ON. SHE'S A SWEET OLD LADY

OH, I'M SORRY. I THOUGHT YOU MEANT THE SAME AUNT GUSSIE WHO WAS KICKED OUT OF THE MARINES FOR UNNECESSARY ROUGHNESS!

© 1988 United Feature Syndicate, Inc.

© 1988 United Feature Syndicate, Inc.

© 1988 United Feature Syndicate, Inc.

RELENTLESS IN HIS PURSUIT OF FOOD, THE SHARK SCOURS THE OCEAN FLOOR

ABOVE HIM HE SPIES THE SHADOWY SILHOUETTE OF A LIFE RAFT WITH A LONE SURVIVOR!

JIM DAVIS 5-7

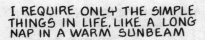

© 1988 United Feature Syndicate, Inc.

I CAN SEE TODAY IS GOING TO BE A REAL YAWN A MINUTE

JIM DAVIS 5-14

ONE THING I LIKE ABOUT LETHARGY...

© 1988 United Feature Syndicate, Inc.

YOU DON'T HAVE TO WORK AT IT

JIM DAVIS

5-21

© 1988 United Feature Syndicate, Inc.

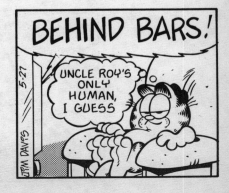

© 1988 United Feature Syndicate, Inc.

© 1988 United Feature Syndicate, Inc.

© 1988 United Feature Syndicate, Inc.

© 1988 United Feature Syndicate, Inc.

JIM DAVIS 7-14

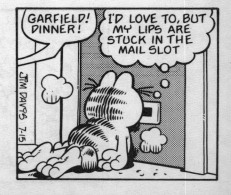

GARFIELD! DINNER!

I'D LOVE TO, BUT MY LIPS ARE STUCK IN THE MAIL SLOT

JIM DAVIS 7-15

7-16

© 1988 United Feature Syndicate, Inc.

GARFIELD!

JIM DAVIS 7-19

THE MUMMY AWAKENS FROM
A SLEEP OF 3000 YEARS

© 1988 United Feature Syndicate, Inc.

AND SETS HIS SNOOZE ALARM
FOR ANOTHER CENTURY

JIM DAVIS 7-20

7-28

JIM DAVIS 8-2

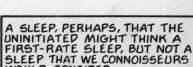

JIM DAVIS 8-18

JIM DAVIS   8-19

OTHER GARFIELD BOOKS IN THIS SERIES

No. 1	Garfield The Great Lover	£2.50
No. 2	Garfield Why Do You Hate Mondays?	£2.50
No. 3	Garfield Does Pooky Need You?	£2.50
No. 4	Garfield Admit It, Odie's OK!	£2.50
No. 5	Garfield Two's Company	£2.50
No. 6	Garfield What's Cooking?	£2.50
No. 7	Garfield Who's Talking?	£2.50
No. 8	Garfield Strikes Again	£2.50
No. 9	Garfield Here's Looking At You	£2.50
No. 10	Garfield We Love You Too	£2.50
No. 11	Garfield Here We Go Again	£2.50
No. 12	Garfield Life and Lasagne	£2.50
No. 13	Garfield In The Pink	£2.50
No. 14	Garfield Just Good Friends	£2.50
No. 15	Garfield Plays It Again	£2.50
No. 16	Garfield Flying High	£2.50
No. 17	Garfield On Top Of The World	£2.50
No. 19	Garfield Going Places	£2.50
No. 20	Garfield Le Magnifique!	£2.50
No. 21	Garfield In The Fast Lane	£2.50
No. 22	Garfield In Tune	£2.50
No. 23	Garfield The Reluctant Romeo	£2.50
No. 24	Garfield With Love From Me To You	£2.50
No. 25	Garfield A Gift For You	£2.50
No. 26	Garfield Great Impressions	£2.50

GARFIELD GALLERIES

Garfield Gallery No. 1	£4.95
Garfield Gallery No. 2	£4.95
Garfield Gallery No. 3	£4.95
Garfield Gallery No. 4	£4.95
Garfield Gallery No. 5	£4.95
Garfield Gallery No. 6	£4.95
Garfield Gallery No. 7	£4.95

GARFIELD COMIC ALBUMS

No. 1	Sitting Pretty	£3.99
No. 2	Words Of Wisdom	£3.99

COLOUR TV SPECIALS

Here Comes Garfield	£2.95
Garfield On The Town	£2.95
Garfield In The Rough	£2.95
Garfield In Disguise	£2.95
Garfield In Paradise	£2.95
Garfield Goes To Hollywood	£2.95
A Garfield Christmas	£2.95
Garfield's Thanksgiving	£2.95
Garfield's Feline Fantasies	£2.95
Garfield Gets A Life	£2.95
Garfield's Night Before Christmas	£3.95
Garfield's Tales Of Mystery	£3.95
Garfield's Scary Tales	£3.95
Garfield The Easter Bunny?	£3.95
Garfield Best Ever	£4.95
Garfield Selection	£5.95
Garfield His 9 Lives	£5.95
Garfield Diet Book	£4.95
Garfield Exercise Book	£4.95
Garfield Book Of Love	£2.99
The Garfield Birthday Book	£3.99

All these books are available at your local bookshop or newsagent, or can be ordered direct from the publisher. Just tick the titles you require and fill in the form below. Prices and availability subject to change without notice.

Ravette Books, PO Box 11, Falmouth, Cornwall, TR10 9EN.

Please send a cheque or postal order for the value of the book, and add the following for postage and packing:
UK including BFPO – £1.00 per order.
OVERSEAS, including EIRE – £2.00 per order.
OR Please debit this amount from my Access/Visa Card (delete as appropriate).

Card Number ☐☐☐☐☐☐☐☐☐☐☐☐☐☐☐☐☐☐

AMOUNT £ ....   EXPIRY DATE ....

SIGNED ....

NAME ....

ADDRESS ....